My Love Affair: Thorns and Roses
―――――――――――――――――――――――――

Natalia Lazarus

NATALIA LAZARUS

My Love Affair:
Thorns and Roses

**ODE TO AN
UNFORGETTABLE
ROMANCE**

CENTRAL PARK SOUTH PUBLISHING
NEW YORK CITY, NEW YORK

Copyright © 2021 by Natalia Lazarus

All rights reserved under International and Pan-American Copyright Conventions. No part of this publication may be reproduced, distributed or transmitted in any form or by any means, without prior written permission, except in the case of reprints in the context of reviews.

The author gratefully acknowledges permission to reprint selected artwork from the oeuvre of Pablo Picasso, reprinted courtesy of The Estate of Pablo Picasso, Artists Rights Society (ARS), New York, and Art Resource, New York.

Publisher: Central Park South Publishing
website: www.centralparksouthpublishing.com

Publisher's Note: This is a work of fiction. Names, characters, places, and incidents are a product of the author's imagination. Locales and public names are sometimes used for atmospheric purposes. Any resemblance to actual people, living or dead, or to businesses, companies, events, institutions, or locales is completely coincidental.

Book Layout: Jonathan Miertschin
Jacket Design: Monterey Bay Design
Cover Photo and Inner Jacket Photo: Harry Langdon

My Love Affair: Thorns and Roses: Ode to an Unforgettable Romance by Natalia Lazarus. -- 1st ed, Copyright © Natalia Lazarus 2021

Library of Congress Control Number: 2021914832

Enjoy *My Love Affair: Thorns and Roses: Ode to an Unforgettable Romance* as an audio book narrated by the author, in English, Spanish, and French, wherever audio books are sold.

ISBN 978-1-7363134-9-7

A Picasso

A Play by
Jeffrey Hatcher

Natalia Lazarus

Charles Fathy

THÉÂTRE de NESLE
8 rue de Nesle 75006 Paris

FOREWORD
by Jeffrey Hatcher (Playwright)

Natalia Lazarus is an actress and director, so it comes as no surprise that her poetry collection, *My Love Affair: Thorns and Roses*, is actually a drama, with the kind of twists and turns one associates with a well-constructed stage play.

It's also meta-theatrical, because the love affair she chronicles in her spare yet heartbreaking verses takes place while she is directing and performing in a play – mine, as it happens - *A Picasso*.

Lazarus' journey takes her from sun baked beaches and candlelit dinners to those shadow realms called backstage, in the wings and behind the curtain. The book is warm and witty, a page-turner, and a love story.

PREFACE

I began my career as an actress. The craft of acting informs everything I do, write, direct, produce, this is, in fact, my life.

In 2013, my mother died. No one knew she was dying. We all thought mom was just recovering from back surgery. I was in the hospital with her, incessantly and annoyingly on my cell phone, making preparations for the production of the play, *A Picasso*, by Jeffrey Hatcher, to be performed in the South of France and eventually in Paris and Los Angeles.

I remember my mother telling one of the nurses in her heavy Latin-accented English, "Ah my daughter always searching for more, nothing good enough for her. Now she goes to do play in France. In French. Hollywood not enough."

For the next four years, I went on to direct and act in *A Picasso*, in English and French. The journey was exhilarating. Every performance of playing *Mademoiselle Fischer*, the Nazi Cultural Attaché, brought in to interrogate and destroy *Pablo Picasso* in Occupied Paris, was emotionally shattering.

In the pre-production phase of the Parisian production, I met a man who whiplashed my life into a stunning love affair that took us from Paris, to San Francisco, to Malibu, to Las Vegas, to Santa Barbara, to New York, and back, and back again. In this time period, I wrote the poetry that you find in this book, *My Love Affair: Thorns and Roses*.

The poetry was never meant as an artistic endeavor. It just flowed out of me as I was in a constant state of angst and turmoil. I was living two lives, *Mademoiselle Fischer's* and my own. *Mademoiselle Fischer* had Hatcher's text to express how she felt. The poetry was the incessant monologue purging itself from my heart.

When the love affair was over, so was the poetry from that moment in time. I didn't do anything with the poems. They just sat in the confines of my computer.

Then, one day, I began writing the screenplay, *A Year in Picasso*. Much like the poetry, it just flowed out of me. As I wrote, I remembered the poems and used excerpts from them for the voiceover of the main character, *Emma*. The device revealed her emotional state. Life becomes Art?

My fiancé, Tom, made fun of me and called me Trumbo, referencing the 1940's screenwriter, Dalton Trumbo, who used elaborate cards and diagrams to create his scripts. Tom witnessed my outlines and diagrams; more importantly, how I inserted excerpts from *A Picasso*, into my screenplay.

When I was finally done with the 165 page manuscript, Tom walked by the printer and began to read. He pointed to one of the poetry excerpts and said, "What is this?" "Oh, just some poetry," I replied, dismissively. When he was done reading the screenplay, *A Year in Picasso*, he asked me if he could have a copy of all the poems. I hesitated, as they were poems inspired by another man.

Reluctantly, months later, I printed them all out and gave them to him. I didn't want him to think I was hiding anything. When he was done he said, "Your poems moved me and made me cry. I think they tell a story and they should be a book".

Natalia Lazarus

A Moment in Time...

A Moment in My Heart...

INTRODUCTION

This is how my story began… I was living in Paris in the Troisième arrondissement between La Place de la Bastille and La Place de la République. Several times a week, I walked to my ballet class at the Centre de danse du Marais and on my return home I would always pass the Musée Picasso on the rue de Thorigny.

The Musée Picasso had been under renovation for five years and it was scheduled to reopen in the fall of 2014. I would stand at the gates in awe of the 17th century building once known as the Hotel Salé. That was when I started my love affair with Pablo Picasso. I knew nothing about him. Only that he was a celebrated painter, of course.

One of my colleagues predicted that around the world, 2014 would be an explosive year for Pablo Picasso. She suggested that I create something in my *Promenade Playhouse* theatre in Los Angeles that would commemorate him. Something, which I could then bring to Paris and join in on the party.

I had, in fact, several years prior, become enamored with an amazing two-character play called, *A Picasso*, by Jeffrey Hatcher. I gave it to my colleague, who read it and said, "C'est magnifique!" That's all I needed to hear to get started on my journey.

A Picasso is an intense confrontational drama layered with sensitivity and wit. Sex, art, politics, Nazis, and the classy 20th century icon are all entwined. *Mademoiselle Fischer*, whom I played, is a cultural attaché from Berlin and she has arrested Picasso. She needs him to authenticate three of his pieces, recently "confiscated", by the Nazis from their Jewish owners, for inclusion in a "degenerate art show", curated by Joseph Goebbels.

In the play, we discover that *Mademoiselle Fischer* is an art historian, well versed, not only in the works of Pablo Picasso but of his contemporaries as well. Being a bit of a method actress and director, I proceeded to learn everything I could about Pablo Picasso and his oeuvre. I fell insanely in love with him, much like *Mademoiselle Fischer*.

My entire journey was quite surreal for me. In Paris, I promenaded myself down the same streets and visited the same cafes that Picasso and *Mademoiselle Fischer* would have frequented in 1941, including Picasso's studio on the rue de Saint Augustin. For the Parisian production, we performed at the Théâtre de Nesle, in the Rive Gauche, around the corner from Picasso's studio. To my surprise and delight our performance was greeted with rave reviews and wonderful, enthusiastic audience response.

As I mention in the Preface of this collection, in the year of *A Picasso* in Paris, I had two love affairs. As *Mademoiselle Fischer*, I was madly and desperately in love with Picasso. As myself, I was madly and desperately in love with a dashing, international banker, the gentleman for whom these poems were written.

I had always envisioned *Thorns and Roses* to be a coffee table book with beautiful images, like one would find in an artist's sketchbook. Drawings, wine, and thoughts of love. Once *Thorns and Roses* started to take shape as a book, we couldn't quite get the imagery right and at some point, my beloved publicist said, "Let's just get real Picasso's in the book." And I thought, "Sure, YES! Why not?"

I am so in love with each one of the Picassos that we have selected for this collection and hope that you will have as much delight in them as I have. Each one has been hand picked as either a companion piece for a specific poem or to mark the beginning of each act of my love story, conveying in an image the primal feeling of each act.

Each act in my book is also comprised of a setting and time. The settings are defined as Paris, my second home and where I met the gentleman in question; Malibu, my primary home; San Francisco, my beau's home; and New York City, where I went to college, often do business, and where my lover's wife lived.

In order to come up with the selection of Picasso's for each act, I used his painting time periods to guide the way. The Beyeler Foundation in Switzerland places Picasso's Blue and Rose Period from 1901– 1906.

For *Act One*, I was inspired by Picasso's Rose Period, which is at times classified with the characteristics of joy and romance. The painting *Harlequin and his Companion* has the perfect combination of fun, lightness of spirit, and French coolness to convey the feelings surrounding *The Encounter* with my new beau in Montparnasse.

For *Act Two*, I borrowed from Picasso's Black Period, which is classified as being from 1906 – 1909. For my act entitled, *The Next Step*, the Black Period does not represent darkness but rather a spirit of magic filled with pure and unadulterated love. The painting, *Friendship* blends the highly stylized treatment of the human figure in African sculptures, holding for me the treasured space in love where we feel understood and protected.

The painting, *Girl before a Mirror*, really spoke to me for *Act Three*, *The Questioning*. Painted in 1932 during Picasso's Surrealism Period, the painting depicts the obsessive alternate reality of desire and dreams that can overtake our being when we are in love and wondering if that love will stay with us. Is that love true?

For *Act Four* I used the *The Old Guitarist*, which was painted in 1901 during the Blue Period as Picasso grieved the death of his best friend to suicide. It conveys the sadness and heightened feelings of torment I experienced when I realized there were many broken promises in my love story.

In my journey of learning about Picasso, I discovered that the many women he loved in his lifetime were also his muses. I was particularly fascinated with Dora Maar, the French photographer, painter, and poet who had a romantic relationship with Picasso for nine years.

During his romance with Dora Maar, Picasso maintained his relationship with Marie Thérèse, the mother of his daughter, Maya; creating a rivalry between the two women. Before meeting Picasso, Dora Maar was very confident, led a full life, and was an artist in her own right. Yet, in spite of all her triumphs, she succumbed to Picasso's charm and next to him, seemed to become "the invisible woman."

I identified with Dora Maar, in that I too led a full life, was very confident, and was an artist in my own right, when I met the international banker in Paris. Yet, with each passing day, that confidence lessened, and I too became a tortured woman on the verge of a nervous breakdown.

The Weeping Woman in *Act Five*, *The Unraveling*, is Picasso's depiction of Dora Maar as a tortured, anguished woman. This was the perfect painting to depict the complete and utter desolation I felt when I discovered that our *Camelot*, the idyllic, metaphorical place my lover had created for us, was nothing but a lie.

For *Act Six*, *The Disappointment*, I couldn't think of a better painting than *The Blue Room* to convey regret and mourning. A woman, alone in her room, clearly broken as she bathes herself. On the last day that I ever saw my beau, I took an interminably long shower, as if the water would shed every remnant of the love affair, leaving me fresh and open to new beginnings.

Act Seven, *The Road Back*, takes place in New York City where I was on a business trip right after the breakup and where my ex-beau had gone to reunite with his estranged wife. It took every inch of strength to not succumb to his attempts at contacting me.

It was on this trip that I purposefully decided to let go, forevermore. I got rid of the engagement ring and any hope that we would ever reunite. I literally walked away from his apartment building, from his street, from his life, and went back to living mine.

As I walked on Park Avenue towards the High Line, my scarf fluttered in the wind and I felt peace. The drama, the trauma, it was finally over and new journeys awaited.

Picasso's *Dove of Peace* was chosen in 1949, as an emblem for the First International Peace Conference in Paris, in the aftermath of the Second World War. In 1957, the *Dove of Peace* was used again in a silkscreen scarf created for the Global Festival of Youth, held in Moscow in 1957. That piece is entitled *Moscou*. Peace, youth, new beginnings, and a scarf fluttering in the wind. What better way to end my love story?

The remaining five Picasso's selected for this collection are interspersed throughout, accentuating specific poems in a way that seems naturally obvious. I wrote the poem, *The Dream*, when I first met the banker and everything seemed so perfect, as if my prayers for what I envisioned love could be, had been answered.

While Pablo Picasso was married to his first wife, Olga Khokhlova, the Russian dancer, he fell in love with the seventeen-year-old model, Marie Thérèse Walter. He was forty-five. Marie Thérèse became his mistress for the next eight years, from 1927 – 1935, whilst Olga never gave Picasso the divorce he so much desired.

In 1932, Picasso painted Marie Thérèse in *The Dream*. She had become his young, sleeping muse; and in many other paintings like this one, he portrays her in tranquility, physically attractive, and sexually naïve.

As the banker was much older than I was, I could relate to *The Dream*. During my love affair, I often slept in peace and for long periods of time. I felt happy and safe; albeit, like Marie Thérèse, being very naïve as to all that is involved in a triangulating love affair.

After our encounter in Paris, I visited my beau at his home in San Francisco. During our romance this enchanting city often became our weekend getaway. We had regular activities we enjoyed: jazz at the Ritz Carlton, comedy shows at the Punchline, and dinner in China Beach; however, one of my most vivid memories is visiting the Flower Market on Brannan Street. My beau bought so many flowers. There were vases throughout the house that he prepared all on his own. He especially dedicated to me a gigantic arrangement of red and white roses. This visit to the flower market inspired my poem, *Bouquets of Flowers*. Ironically, many years prior, when I lived in New York City, I had purchased a lithograph of Picasso's *El Ramo de Flores*, painted in 1958. Well, nothing more needed to be explored. Of course, *El Ramo de Flores* fits perfectly with *Bouquets of Flowers*.

One hand gives, as another receives. These hands represent friendship, union, beauty. For me, the feelings expressed in this painting tied in with the strong alliance I felt with my beau and the genuine friendship I was trying to create with his family.

I wrote the poem, *Dinner Alone*, at the restaurant Bui Sushi in Malibu, as I had dinner alone and thought of my beau. *The Absinthe Drinker* painted by Picasso in 1901, seemed like a more than obvious choice to accompany this poem. A woman, who is absorbed in her thoughts, alone, embraces and protects herself with her hands. That is exactly how I felt when my beau departed to sort out his divorce. Alone, unsteady, and deep in thought at the role I had chosen in this love affair. There we were. He, in New York City. I, in Malibu. Together, yet alone…

Picasso's *Mediterranean Landscape*, completed in 1952, once his cubism style was developed, is classified as a kickback into the Crystal Period of Synthetic Cubism. Picasso developed this style of painting with his friend and colleague, Georges Braque, utilizing cut paper fragments, wallpaper, and newspaper to create an assemblage of different forms, thus creating a new whole. The style is playful, light hearted, and lively.

For several years I had been spending glorious summers in the South of France. I vacationed in Nice, Marseille, Saint Paul de Vince, Saint Tropez, Roussillon, Lourmarin, and Ménerbes. It was in the small village of Ménerbes that Picasso bought Dora Maar the house where she was to spend a good portion of her life. After their break up, it was in this home where she recovered from her nervous breakdown as he continued to torment her. Finally she was able to reconnect with herself and her art.

In my journeys, I was always delighted to return to Cannes, where I had first visited when I was a student at the University of London, and where I completed my thesis film, *Darkroom*. Picasso also lived in Cannes, at the Villa La Californie, with his last wife, Jacqueline Roque.

My home base was the beautiful town of Aix en Provence. I lived right next to Mont Saint Victoire, the glorious mountain that Cezanne painted over one hundred times and where I often went hiking. Already heavily involved in my journey with Picasso, I visited on several occasions, another one of Picasso's homes, the Château of Vauvenargues, which he bought in 1958. Located in the outskirts of Aix, this is also where Picasso is buried.

When the play *A Picasso* got picked up to tour in Avignon, Bonnieux, and Carpintras, it only enhanced my love affair with the South of France, which coincided with Picasso's love of the French Riviera towns. The painting *Mediterranean Landscape* captured for me that love and fun in the sun feeling that came with sipping rosé and long summer lunches in the Cote d'Azur. *Mediterranean Landscape* was to be the perfect companion for my poem *Summer in Antibes*.

The final Picasso in my collection is *La toilette*, painted in 1906, at the end of the Rose Period, in Spain, in the village of Gósol in the Pyrenees, where Picasso and his girlfriend, Fernande Olivier, had gone to spend the summer. In this painting, a woman looks into a mirror held by another woman. She sees herself, as she prepares for what is to come.

I have long admired this painting because it reminds me of what we do before we go on stage and before we go out in public, for that matter. We go through a ritual of cleansing ourselves, preparing ourselves, and even looking at ourselves in ways we may have not done so before. The woman doing her toilette is nude. I identified with her for the last section of the book called, *The Encore*. This painting signifies for me, a rebirth, new beginnings, and a symbol of hope, for the best is yet to come. It seemed to be the perfect Picasso with which to end the book.

In the Rose Period, filled with joy and happiness for the poems, *No More Tears* and *To the Future*. Cheers! For the future is always bright!!

PROGRAMME
MY MOMENTS IN TIME

FOREWORD .... *ix*
PREFACE .... *xi*
INTRODUCTION .... *xvii*
THE PABLO PICASSO GALLERY .... *xxxiv*

PROLOGUE 1

ACT I: THE ENCOUNTER 3
    Scene 1: The Dream 7
    Scene 2: Crazy Love 11
    Scene 3: Happy Holidays 13

ACT II: THE NEXT STEP 17
    Scene 1: Girl Thoughts 21
    Scene 2: Wedding Bells 25
    Scene 3: Our Light 29
    Scene 4: Bouquets of Flowers 33

ACT III: THE QUESTIONING 43
    Scene 1: In Another Time 47
    Scene 2: Dinner Alone 53
    Scene 3: Can't Wait 57
    Scene 4: Love and Affection 61
    Scene 5: Now that You Found Me 65

ACT IV: THE TORMENT 73
   Scene 1: Trio 77
   Scene 2: Twin Flames 83
   Scene 3: Broken Promises 87

ACT V: THE UNRAVELING 91
   Scene 1: Summer in Antibes 95
   Scene 2: Camelot 101
   Scene 3: Thought We Had Something .. 105

ACT VI: THE DISAPPOINTMENT 109
   Scene 1: Without You 113
   Scene 2: I'll Miss You 117
   Scene 3: My Dreams Up in Smoke 121
   Scene 4: So Very Sad 123

ACT VII: THE ROAD BACK 127
   Scene 1: Away from You 131
   Scene 2: Reflections 133

FINALE 136
   My Curtain Call 139

ENCORE 143
   Part 1: No More Tears 145
   Part 2: To the Future 146

CAST PARTY/ACKNOWLEDGEMENTS 149
EPILOGUE 153
IMAGE CREDITS 158

Portrait of Pablo Picasso, 1908, by Anonymous

My Love Affair: Thorns & Roses

THE PABLO PICASSO GALLERY

Harlequin and his Companion 2

The Dream 6

Friendship 16

El Ramo de Flores 32

Girl before a Mirror 42

The Absinthe Drinker 52

The Old Guitarist 72

The Weeping Woman 90

Mediterranean Landscape 95

The Blue Room 108

Dove of Peace 126

La toilette 142

VERY SPECIAL THANKS TO...
The Estate of Pablo Picasso, Artists Rights Society (ARS), New York, and Art Resource, New York.

*A very special thanks to
Gene Schwam,
whose invaluable input
is responsible for moving
the creation of this book
forward.*

For Tom, who stayed...

Natalia Lazarus

Prologue

Moments of love
Found and lost

From extraordinary joy
To despairing uncertainty

Extreme sorrow
Followed by new beginnings

Thus is my journey
During a moment in time

A moment with you
Engraved in my heart

Natalia Lazarus

Pablo Picasso
Harlequin and his Companion

Picasso, Pablo (1881-1973) @ ARS, NY
Harlequin and his Companion (The Two Saltimbanques), 1901.
Found in the collection of the State A Pushkin Museum of Fine Arts, Moscow
Pushkin Museum of Fine Arts, Moscow, Russia
Photo Credit: HIP / Art Resource, NY
© 2021 Estate of Pablo Picasso / Artists Rights Society (ARS), New York

ACT I
The Encounter

Scene 1 .... **The Dream**

Scene 2 .... **Crazy Love**

Scene 3 .... **Happy Holidays**

Natalia Lazarus

JOY

ACT I

The Setting:

A FABULOUS apartment, in the RIVE GAUCHE section of PARIS

The Time:

FALL 2014, as the FÊTES DES VENDANGES are celebrated

Natalia Lazarus

Pablo Picasso
The Dream

Picasso, Pablo (1881-1973) @ ARS, NY
The Dream (Le Rêve), Boisgeloup, January 24, 1932.
Oil on canvas, 130 x 98 cm.
Photo Credit: Erich Lessing / Art Resource, NY
© 2021 Estate of Pablo Picasso / Artists Rights Society (ARS), New York

ACT I: Scene 1

The Dream

I must have dreamed you, surely
Or I must have known you in another time

I have been looking for you
    My whole life
    All over the world

Thinking of you
    Longing for you

As a child
    As a girl
    As a woman

Laughing with you
    Dancing with you
    Living with you

continued...

You see
> All of me
> So easily
> So quickly
> So lovingly

I must have dreamed you, surely
Or I must have known you in another time

Now you are here
> Laughing with me
> Dancing with me
> Living with me

The child
> The boy
> The man

I see
> All of you
> So easily
> So quickly
> So lovingly

I must have dreamed you, surely
Or I must have known you in another time

My hand
> In your hand

My eyes
> In your eyes

My heart
> In your heart

Child with Child
> Boy with Girl
> Man with Woman

You and Me
> Finally
> In the same dream

Natalia Lazarus

ACT I: Scene 2
Crazy Love

An outcast
That is what I feel like
That is what I am

Yet
You understood
Exactly who I am

You saw me
You needed me
You loved me

Natalia Lazarus

I will walk with you

Where others never have...

ACT I: Scene 3
Happy Holidays

Happy Holidays
> To a man who gives so much
> Bringing out the best in us
> To flourish by the bunch

To the dream man
> May you be filled with love
> Pride and joy
> For all you have created

To all of you
> The baby
> The child
> The man

continued...

The one I cherish
    Honour
    Love
    In whom I see
    All I have ever wished for

The Dream Man
    Father
    Brother
    Friend
    Lover

I will walk with you
> Where others never have
> I will hold you
> Support you
> Nurture you

Never ever
> Leave you
> I am with you
> Dearest angel
> Love of my life

Natalia Lazarus

Pablo Picasso
Friendship

Picasso, Pablo (1881 -1973) @ ARS, NY
Friendship, 1907-1908.
Pushkin Museum of Fine Arts, Moscow, Russia
Photo Credit: HIP / Art Resource, NY
© 2021 Estate of Pablo Picasso / Artists Rights Society (ARS), New York

ACT II
The Next Step

Scene 1 .... **Girl Thoughts**

Scene 2 .... **Wedding Bells**

Scene 3 .... **Our Light**

Scene 4 .... **Bouquets of Flowers**

Natalia Lazarus

MAGIC

ACT II

The Setting:

A cold, multilevel house in the GLEN PARK section of SAN FRANCISCO

The Time:

WINTER 2015, as the FLOWER MARKET FAIR opens

Just you and me...

Could it really be?

ACT II: Scene 1
Girl Thoughts

M y stomach is in knots
    Don't know what to say
    Or what is to come
    So much time has gone by
    Can I keep you by my side

I long for your love
    Yet you are so far away
    Don't know what to say
    There will be no more 3
    We must now be 2 for tea

continued...

We are official
    We can disclose our romance
    Hiding is over
    Convenient answers unnecessary
    We are finally exclusive

The circle of suitors
    Will be disbanded
    I have found the man
    Whom I will follow
    Into eternity

I feel giddy
    Nervous
    Vulnerable
    My heart palpitates
    I wait

I prepare myself
    Finally
    Back in your arms
    Having an instinct
    That all will be well

Needing desperately
    Your touch
    Your breath
    As it blends with mine
    Becoming one

       Us
       One
       Us

Just you and me
    Could it really be

I am next to be wed...

ACT II: Scene 2
Wedding Bells

I went to my friend's wedding
Hoping that's where you'd be heading

All the way till ten
I danced with other men

I would have liked to waltz with you
To not feel so terribly blue

In the open air
What a pair

continued...

Will it be you in my bed?

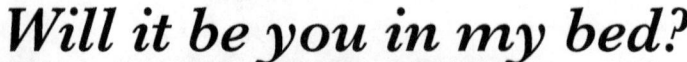

Under the starry night
All is bright

Feeling the beating of your heart
Your breath in part

I catch the bouquet
At the Brasserie Fouquet

I am next to be wed
Will it be you in my bed?

ACT II: Scene 3
Our Light

May the love bursting through my being
Reach you through the electric air

Against the crashing waves
I offer my heart
I hope
I pray

With stars sparkling
Effervescing
May a river of awakening
Surround you

continued...

May you have
At long last
The courage to end
What has long been dead

May you return
Energized
Confident
On the path to follow

With new life pouring
In love adoring
Flowing back
Into our singing symmetry

May the love bursting through my being
Reach you through the electric air

Natalia Lazarus

Pablo Picasso
El Ramo de Flores

Picasso, Pablo (1881-1973) @ ARS, NY
EL RAMO DE FLORES - 1958.
LITOGRAFIA. Author: RUIZ PICASSO, PABLO
Location: PRIVATE COLLECTION
Photo Credit: Album / Art Resource, NY
© 2021 Estate of Pablo Picasso / Artists Rights Society (ARS), New York

ACT II: Scene 4
Bouquets of Flowers

I prepared
    My own bouquets of flowers tonight

    Not bought
    Just random flowers
    Given to me by a friend

    I had to cut them
    Nurture them
    Give them new life

    They weren't for a dinner party
    Nor for anything in particular
    Just leftovers

    Orphans
    Like me I suppose
    An affirmation
    That I exist

continued...

I prepared
>   My own bouquets of flowers tonight

>   I didn't have many vases
>   Just a few
>   Here and there

>   The strangest thing happened
>   Imaginary conversations
>   With your wife

>   Am I going mad
>   Did I pick this lad
>   Is this a joke
>   Or a dream from which I woke

I prepared
>   My own bouquets of flowers tonight

>   I took 3 puffs from a vape
>   As I stared at the 76 sign
>   Through our opened drape

>   The numbers 7 and 6
>   Float ominously in the air
>   Is it some sort of dare

I prepared
>My own bouquets of flowers tonight

>I am here
>In our home
>Alone
>With the crashing waves

>You are
>Somewhere up north
>In a hearth
>That has lost its warmth

I prepared
>My own bouquets of flowers tonight

>Not during my time
>I know
>In her time
>Your love flourished no more

>NOW
>At exactly this time
>I am in the middle of a family
>That is not mine

continued...

I prepared
    My own bouquets of flowers tonight

    I felt like Cinderella
    I could see it
    Camelot at last

    I get to walk off with the King
    I know
    It must all be done
    Before the midnight ring

    The castle is there
    I know
    Camelot is within reach
    I know

    Will the Queen Mother
    With her children torment me
    Or will they embrace me

My Love Affair: Thorns & Roses

I prepared
>My own bouquets of flowers tonight

>Red roses for you and Aaron
>Pink tulips for Hanna
>Green orchids for June

>I love you
>I honour you
>I consent to your every term

I prepared
>My own bouquets of flowers tonight

>NOW
>A WHOLE NEW CHAPTER

>>You are
>>My father
>>My brother
>>My friend
>>My lover

continued...

I prepared
>My own bouquets of flowers tonight

>NOW
>A WHOLE NEW CHAPTER

>>Your wife
>>Is my mother
>>My sister
>>My companion
>>My friend

I prepared
>My own bouquets of flowers tonight

>NOW
>A WHOLE NEW CHAPTER

>>Your children
>>Are my children
>>The ones I never had
>>My brother
>>My sister
>>My companions
>>My friends

I prepared
>My own bouquets of flowers tonight

>You are my healing
>My path to enlightenment
>To love
>As I have never known it
>My fantasy
>My reality
>Camelot at last

I prepared
>My own bouquets of flowers tonight

>Please
>Hold my hand
>As you take me through the gates
>Lend me your arm
>With the utmost of charm
>To help me withstand
>The unknown strand

continued...

I prepared
> My own bouquets of flowers tonight

> I feel scared
> At odds
> Tears flood my eyes
> As I wait for you
> Yet again

I prepared
> My own bouquets of flowers tonight

> Off to Camelot you say
> What a strange
> Mysterious
> Magical place
> This has all become

I prepared
> My own bouquets of flowers tonight

>> And I prayed

Natalia Lazarus

Pablo Picasso
Girl before a Mirror

Picasso, Pablo (1881 -1973) @ ARS, NY
Girl before a Mirror. Boisgeloup, March 1932.
Oil on canvas, 64 x 51 ¼" (162.3 x 130.2 cm).
Gift of Mrs. Simon Guggenheim.
Digital Image @ The Museum of Modern Art/ Licensed by SCALA / Art Resource, NY
© 2021 Estate of Pablo Picasso / Artists Rights Society (ARS), New York

ACT III
The Questioning

Scene 1 ...... **In Another Time**

Scene 2 ...... **Dinner Alone**

Scene 3 ...... **Can't Wait**

Scene 4 ...... **Love and Affection**

Scene 5 ...... **Now that You Found Me**

Natalia Lazarus

OBSESSION

ACT III

The Setting:

A beachfront condo on BROAD BEACH in MALIBU

The Time:

SPRING 2015, as the TIDE begins to swell

ACT III: Scene 1
In Another Time

Tick tock

Another clock
2 years

TICK TOCK

Banker terms
24 months
And we'll know

I feel like an investment
Are the terms agreeable

TICK TOCK
TICK TOCK

continued...

What is the profit margin
Don't sign on the dotted line
Just yet

TICK TOCK
TICK TOCK

Diversify perhaps
One never knows
Fluctuating markets

TICK TOCK
TICK TOCK

6 months accrued
18 to go
Will I mature

TICK TOCK
TICK TOCK

Will I be sold
Traded
Bought by another

TICK TOCK
TICK TOCK

Is there a fine for early withdrawal
Does the investment double
If I just stay put

TICK TOCK
TICK TOCK

We'll find out
In 24 months
All these darn clocks

TICK TOCK
TICK TOCK

continued...

Most investments like these
You say
Fizzle out in 24 months
If ours doesn't
Will there be yet another clock

TICK TOCK
TICK TOCK

Doesn't it stress you out
That there is a ticking clock
When the buzzer goes off
At 24 months
What will have been measured

TICK TOCK
TICK TOCK

Our time together
Our bodies entwined
Our mounting passion
Our dreams in fruition
Our love come true

Tick Tock

Still counting
Can't wait
For the
TICKING TOCK
To end

TOCK TOCK TOCK
When will OUR clock
Truly begin

TICK TOCK
TICK TOCK

Natalia Lazarus

Pablo Picasso
The Absinthe Drinker

Picasso, Pablo (1881 -1973) @ ARS, NY
The Absinthe Drinker. 1901.
Oil on canvas, 73 x 54 cm.
Photo Credit: Scala / Art Resource, NY
© 2021 Estate of Pablo Picasso / Artists Rights Society (ARS), New York

Act III: Scene 2
Dinner Alone

I was you tonight
I was you and with you

Dinner alone
Out and about

Across from me
A single mom
2 kids
Still
Alone
I could tell

Next to me
A family of 3
Mom and Dad
Definitely apart

continued...

He on his cell phone
She looking out
Alone
I could tell

Perhaps that was once you
With your wife and kids
Alone
Nonetheless

I was definitely alone
No mystery there

I read my book
Sipped my drink
Nibbled my food
Thought of you

I wondered how many times
You had done dinner alone
Whether accompanied
Or not

I wondered
WHY

I thought of you
On the other side of the country
Doing the same perhaps
Being alone

I wondered
WHY

I am here now
So are you

We could stop being alone
Stop imagining conversations
Stop thinking about the future
Stop being afraid

Couldn't we just have dinner
Tonight
Tomorrow
And every night after that

Take me...

ACT III: Scene 3
Can't Wait

I would jump on a plane for you
NOW

Can't wait
To be with you
If only for 2 nights
No ego
No questions

I would jump on a plane for you
NOW

continued...

Make me yours.

I accept
It is as the universe desires

Can't wait
To wrap my body around yours
Your mouth on my mouth

My body melting
Take me
Make me yours

I would jump on a plane for you
NOW

ACT III: Scene 4
Love and Affection

Love and affection
    Could it really be
    How could we know
    Did we just go with the flow

How could we be
    So in tune
    Could we really be
    Like flowers in bloom

continued...

I am so very drawn to you
>   Your body
>   Your smell
>   Your eyes

I desire you
>   Like no other
>   So many candidates
>   But none YOU

You make my body palpitate
>   My breath falter
>   My heart skip
>   Like no other

Bring back your magic
    Don't let me forget
    Grab me
    Hold me

LOVE ME

I love you
    Desperately
    Childishly
    Greedily

Please
    Come back to me

Natalia Lazarus

Will you just love me...

And never look back?

ACT III: Scene 5
Now that You Found Me

Now that you found me
    Will you keep me

The universe whisked me to you
    You accepted
    You made room for me
    You seduced me
    Then you asked me to stay

You'd been looking for me
    I accepted
    You felt true
    I was so relieved
    Then you asked me to stay

continued...

Now that you found me
> Will you keep me

Beyond lust
> Unexplainable
> New
> Pure
> Special

You are
> Addicting
> Intense
> Perfect
> As if you were made just for me

I too had been searching
> For the warmth you provide
> Your comforting arms
> Your desirous want
> As if you were made just for me

Now that you found me
>   I search for you
>   Long for you
>   Desire you
>   Need you
>   Specifically
>   Unequivocally

Now that you found me
>   Will it always be like this
>   Always parting
>   Always craving each other
>   Like famished children
>   Desperately
>   Regretfully

continued...

Now that you found me
    Will the heartache
    Of not truly having you

STOP

Will the longing

STOP

Will the imaginary conversations

STOP

Now that you found me
    Will I stop wondering
    What you are doing
    If you miss me
    If you love me
    Will I

STOP

Now that you found me
> Will you stop
> Being scared
> Resigned
> Torn
> Will you

> STOP

Now that you found me
> We aspire for next time
> Will it always be like this
> Or will next time
> Become forever time

Now that you found me
> Will you just
> Take me
> Love me
> And never look back

continued...

Now that you found me
    Will you walk through the door
    Will you make me your bride
    Will you finally be mine
    Will I finally be yours

Now that you found me
    I heard you
    Though it took worlds

    I found you
    Though it took years

    I finally have you
    Though it took many tears

Now that you found me
>   I love you
>   Like I have loved no other
>   Let's create a new home
>   For our souls
>   For us

Now that you found me...

Natalia Lazarus

Pablo Picasso
The Old Guitarist

Picasso, Pablo (1881 -1973) @ ARS, NY
The Old Guitarist, late 1903-early 1904.
Oil on panel, 48 3/8 x 32 ½ in. (122.9 x 82.6 cm.)
Helen Birch Bartlett Memorial Collection, 1926.253
Photo Credit: The Art Institute of Chicago / Art Resource, NY
© 2021 Estate of Pablo Picasso / Artists Rights Society (ARS), New York

ACT IV
The Torment

Scene 1 .... **Trio**

Scene 2 .... **Twin Flames**

Scene 3 .... **Broken Promises**

Natalia Lazarus

FRAGMENTS

ACT IV

The Setting:

The beachfront condo in MALIBU

The Time:

EARLY SUMMER 2015, as rogue WAVES suddenly surface

ACT IV: Scene 1
Trio

We are
3
We are
1

To be with you
One must
Accept
3

One must
Accept
Us

continued...

You
Me
Her

Her
You
Me

Me
Her
You

It cannot be escaped
Denied
Forgotten
You go to her
You come to me

You
Me
HER

A vicious circle
3
Ever present
The phone calls
The trips

HER

Burn her!

Patience
Breathe

3
A splinter tearing through my skin
3
A knife piercing through my heart
3

continued...

How can I get rid of 3
How can I make 3
= 2

ONLY YOU CAN

The thought persists
The question persists
The dream persists

One day
It will be 2
You
And
ME

No thoughts
No questions
No regrets

Just
2
The dream comes true

*Against the wind
we found each other...*

ACT IV: Scene 2

Twin Flames

My twin flame
  Against the wind
  We found each other
  Without you
  Our flame will die

My twin flame
  Alive
  Nurturing
  Glowing

continued...

My twin flame
    We keep each other warm
    Without you
    Our flame will die

My twin flame
    Keep our fire
    I need you
    I cannot do it
    Without you

We are twin flames
    Burning
    Without you
    Our flame will die

Why have you taken me for granted...

My Love Affair: Thorns & Roses

ACT IV: Scene 3
Broken Promises

You said I could call anytime
For you and her were over

When I did
You said
God forbid

We'll have to do this
Another time

No goodnight graciousness
No plea asking for my patience

Why have you taken me for granted
Is your attention elsewhere planted

continued...

Natalia Lazarus

Is your attention elsewhere planted?

I feel hurt and humiliated
The obedient princess
Burnt and annihilated

I should have morphed
Into a Queen
Ordered - NO

I FORBID it
To her
You are not to go

Pablo Picasso
The Weeping Woman

Picasso, Pablo (1881 -1973) @ ARS, NY
The Weeping Woman (Femme en pleures). 1937. Oil on canvas, 60.8 x 50.0 cm. Accepted by HM Government in lieu of tax with additional payment (Grant-in-Aid) made with assistance from the National Heritage Memorial Fund, the Art Fund and the Friends of the Tate Gallery 1987.
@ Tate, London / Art Resource, NY
© 2021 Estate of Pablo Picasso / Artists Rights Society (ARS), New York

ACT V
The Unraveling

Scene 1 ..... **Summer in Antibes**

Scene 2 ..... **Camelot**

Scene 3 ..... **Thought We Had Something**

Natalia Lazarus

ACT V

The Setting:

The beachfront condo in MALIBU

The Time:

LATE SUMMER 2015, as the embracing **SEA** becomes one's only companion

Natalia Lazarus

Pablo Picasso
Mediterranean Landscape

Picasso, Pablo (1881-1973) @ ARS, NY
Mediterranean Landscape, 1952.
Photo Credit: Scala / Art Resource, NY
© 2021 Estate of Pablo Picasso / Artists Rights Society (ARS), New York

My Love Affair: Thorns & Roses

ACT V: Scene 1
Summer in Antibes

I look out at the sea
> I feel like the poor girl
> Under the palm tree

Left alone
> As you wander off
> With HER

You and Queen Bee
> On the sea
> In Antibes

What is a princess to do
> Mourn and weep
> It is what princesses do
> When their prince goes

continued...

As you are in Antibes
    I will long and pray for your return
    It is what naive princesses do
    When their prince goes

I will one day be Queen too
    My mother said
    It is my birthright
    Times two

Once I have earned it
    As my kingdom flourishes
    My people
    Will crown me Queen too

Will you then be my King
    Will you leave Queen One
    Crowning me Queen Two

Your Queen was untrue
    In another time
    Off with her head
    Is what would have been said

Summer in Antibes
    Where I can't be
    I feel like the poor girl
    Under the palm tree

What is a princess to do
    Mourn and weep
    It is what princesses do
    When their prince goes

As her breaking heart gasps
    She will remember who she is
    For one day
    She will be Queen too

continued...

Natalia Lazarus

Summer in Antibes will one day be mine...

She will force herself
    To hold her head high
    Though poor and alone
    She will be Queen too

She will embrace her mission
    She will find her strength
    Through her broken heart
    She will remember who she is

She will wipe her last tear
    She will fulfill her destiny
    She will rule without fear

Knowing Summer in Antibes
    Will one day be hers too

Natalia Lazarus

Camelot it is NOT!

ACT V: Scene 2
Camelot

I feel
Angry
Hurt
Naïve

I normally
Kick
Fight
Scream

Camelot you said
I went right ahead
We will all live in peace
At Camelot you said

continued...

I suspended disbelief
Did as I was told
Only to be laughed at
For being so bold

Queen Bee cancelled
Didn't honour the agreement
Not at all
A Camelotian like achievement

In fact
Camelot is a deceiving pact
Created to disarm me
For attack

It has all been for naught
For you
Her
And Camelot are rot

ACT V: Scene 3
Thought We Had Something

Y ou told me so many stories
I wonder if I shared with you
As many as you shared with me

I know your past
Your youth
The boy within

Do you know my past
My youth
The girl within

I regret not having more time
Sitting on the veranda
Relaxing and sipping wine

continued...

I'm resentful and undone
You gave her 30 summers
You didn't even give me one

I miss you
So much pleasure
So much comfort

I really thought we had something

Love
We almost had it
True love

You chose to withhold
Creating tension
Leaving me in the cold

You hurt me
Hurt US
Then chose to flee

I really thought we had something

Emptiness
Loss
Broken dreams

I really thought we had something

Something
Something
Nothing

Pablo Picasso
The Blue Room

Picasso, Pablo (1881 -1973) @ ARS, NY
La chambre bleu (Le tub) (The Blue Room). 1901.
Oil on canvas, 51 x 62.5 cm.
Photo Credit: Album / Art Resource, NY
© 2021 Estate of Pablo Picasso / Artists Rights Society (ARS), New York

ACT VI
The Disappointment

Scene 1 .... **Without You**

Scene 2 .... **I'll Miss You**

Scene 3 .... **My Dreams Up in Smoke**

Scene 4 .... **So Very Sad**

Natalia Lazarus

ACT VI

The Setting:

The FABULOUS apartment, in PARIS, NOT quite so fabulous now

The Time:

FALL 2015, as the burnt orange leaves highlight the PATH HOME

I must let you go...

ACT VI: Scene 1
Without You

Heavy air
Hard to move
Unable to get motivated
Without you

Wondering where you are
What you are doing
Thinking
Feeling
Everything so uncertain
Without you

Patience
Yes
Love
Yes
Still painful
Without you

continued...

Knowing you are
Somewhere else
With someone else
Without ME
I am
Without YOU

Our time is precious
Limited
Much of it wasted
Without you

In this angst
In this separation
To believe
To hang on
How can I do it
Without you

Your north star
Your guiding light
Your salvation
Your final love
I cannot be all that
Without you

I am here
Take me
Follow me
Embrace me
Do not leave me
Without you

Hold my hand
Off we go
I AM your final love
Let me LOVE you
I cannot do it
Without you

Come back
Love me
We will nurture each other
Grow together
It is not possible
Without you

ACT VI: Scene 2
I'll Miss You

I feel sad
Though you insist
I shouldn't be
So noble of you

Yet so unfair
To hide my feelings
Lock them up
As if they weren't there

Thoughts of you – Everywhere

Remnants of you
Memories of you
The ghost of you

continued...

I smell your pillow
Attempting to find you
To feel you
To have you

I feel sad – You're gone

Distant
Disconnected
So far away
So sad

Though you're in my heart
My beacon of light
My source of strength

Though I'm so very happy
You were in my life
I am still
Sad

I look out on the Seine
I feel scared
Alone
Sad

Though I may be silly
Though this may be temporary
For today
I feel sad

You are not with me

To ask me to be happy
Is violently cruel
Brutal
For I am so very sad

What am I to do
Feel happy
I don't
I feel sad

Though I'll miss you
This too will pass

For today – I just feel so very sad

Natalia Lazarus

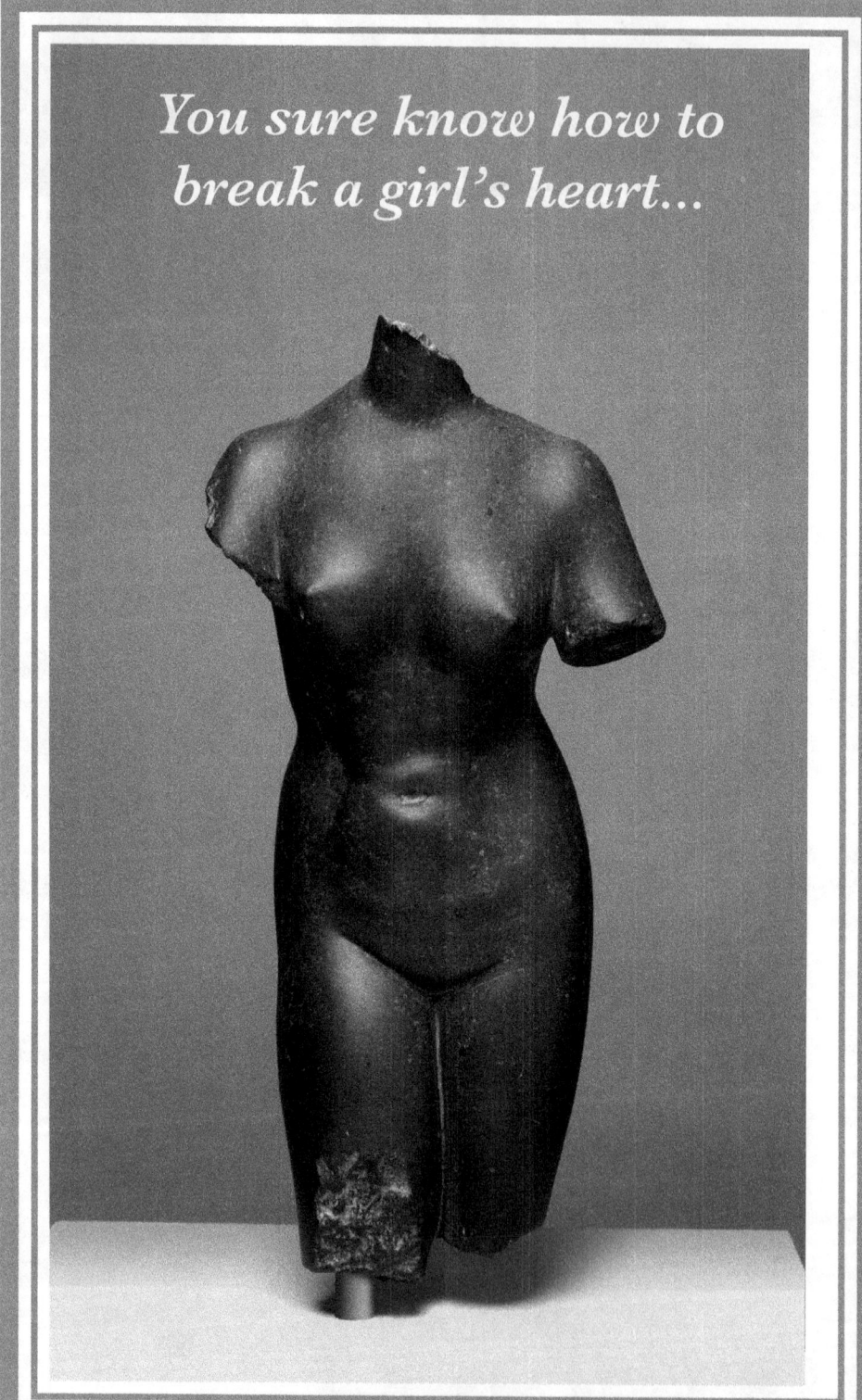

My Love Affair: Thorns & Roses

ACT VI: Scene 3
My Dreams Up in Smoke

I wish I still smoked

It wouldn't be in vain
It would help me with the pain

With the dull ache I feel across my chest
From the memories tucked inside my vest

You said I sure knew how to get a guy's attention
Well you sure know how to break a girl's heart

I wish I still smoked

It wouldn't be in vain
It would help me with the pain

Natalia Lazarus

ACT VI: Scene 4
So Very Sad

I am just so very sad
I mourn for your absence
For the moments not shared

I am just so very sad
For the laughter missed
For the miles that separate us

I am just so very sad
To not have your body next to me
To not have your voice to nurture me

I am just so very sad
To not have your breath to fill me
To not have your kisses to transform me

continued...

Natalia Lazarus

I am just so very sad
My heart is broken
Trembling
Afraid

So very sad
We're not together

So very sad
You chose to leave

So very sad
I can't even
Cry myself to sleep

I am just so very sad

Natalia Lazarus

Pablo Picasso
Dove of Peace

Picasso, Pablo (1881-1973) @ ARS, NY
Moscou. 1957.
Made for the World Youth and Student Festival in Moscow, 1957.
Printed cotton. 77 x 75 cm.
Inv. 2008, 57/01. Kunstbibliothek, Staatliche Museen, Berlin, Germany
Photo Credit: bpk Bildagentur / Art Resource, NY
© 2021 Estate of Pablo Picasso / Artists Rights Society (ARS), New York

ACT VII

The Road Back

Scene 1 .... **Away from You**

Scene 2 .... **Reflections**

Natalia Lazarus

AWAKENING

ACT VII

The Setting:

The **GANSEVOORT HOTEL** on **PARK AVENUE** in **MANHATTAN**

The Time:

WINTER 2016, as the frigid air provides a sobering **REVIVAL**

Natalia Lazarus

ACT VII: Scene 1
Away from You

I was afraid to walk away
I was afraid to break my vow

Didn't know what would come
Just knew it had to be done

Away from you
Away from us

No longer feeling true
Much too blue

I go away from YOU

Natalia Lazarus

I can find myself again...

ACT VII: Scene 2
Reflections

Against the crashing waves
The moonlight beams
My own heart beats

Alone
Yes
Afraid
Yes

Now
SILENCE

continued...

Natalia Lazarus

I can find myself again
Hear myself again
Feel myself again

Now
SILENCE

Just me
Alone
Yes
Afraid
Yes

Within me
ME

Natalia Lazarus

FINALE
My Curtain Call

For the obstacles that torment us
I take my final curtain call

Together
We created US

Nonetheless
I take my final curtain call

continued...

In the deepest of humility
For not being all that you had imagined

In the deepest of sadness
For having lost you

In the deepest of gratitude
For having found you

In the deepest of passion
For I have loved you

A moment with you in my heart
Now the time has come to part

I bow my head
To you at last

Though thrust into the unknown
I find myself again

Thus I take my final curtain call
For above all
Our moment has passed

Natalia Lazarus

Pablo Picasso
La toilette

Picasso, Pablo (1881-1973) @ ARS, NY
La toilette. 1906.
Oil on canvas, support: 59 ½ x 39 inches (151.13 x 99.06 cm); framed:
68 x 48 x 5 inches (172.72 x 121.92 x 12.7 cm).
Albright Knox Art Gallery, Buffalo, New York, New York State, U.S.A.
Photo Credit: Albright Knox Art Gallery / Art Resource, NY
© 2021 Estate of Pablo Picasso / Artists Rights Society (ARS), New York

Encore

Part 1 .... **No More Tears**

Part 2 .... **To the Future**

Natalia Lazarus

ENCORE: Part 1
No More Tears

You said I wasn't rich enough
Without financial security
Which you said you would provide
Then you left

You said next summer
Antibes would be ours
You said so many things
Then you left

I feel awful
Yet thankful
For I grew
In unexpected ways

From the Heavens
My mama whispered
Mourn no more
For YOU will RISE
YOU will FLOURISH

ENCORE: Part 2
To the Future

I will be successful
In spite of all you said

You claimed
I was a sinking ship
Suitable for all to clip
Then you left

I have no more tears
With my sleep no more fears

In spite of all you said
Cheers
For I will RISE
I will FLOURISH

I will be successful
In spite of all you said

There is no turning back
As other journeys begin…

JOIE DE VIVRE

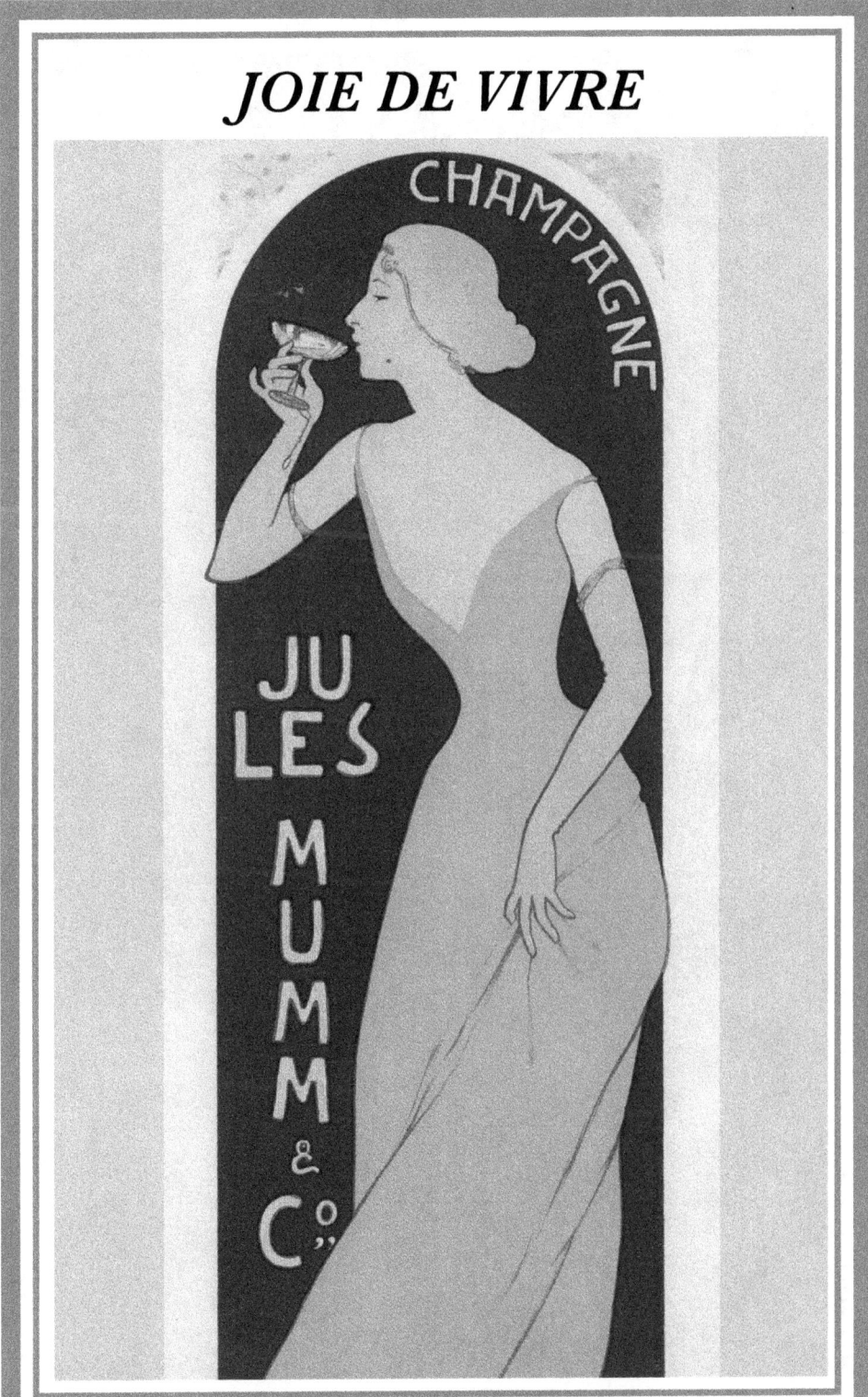

Natalia Lazarus

CAST PARTY / ACKNOWLEDGEMENTS

It takes a village... For those of us who have been part of a theatre or film community, we know how many talented individuals it takes to get the project done. So many have contributed to the production of this book. So many have more responsibility in its creation than they may know.

Linda Langton from Central Park South Publishing has been supportive of my career since she first took interest in another one of my books, *The Actor's Key*. Chuck Hurewitz, my entertainment attorney, who has been a guiding light in my artistic journey, made that introduction for me back in 2013.

My fiancé and partner in life, Tom Waters, has showered me with boundless love, kindness, and unwavering belief in everything I do. It was he, who unbeknownst to me, sent my poetry to Linda in the year of the pandemic.

My friend and colleague, Donna Slatton lived this love story with me. She held my hand, cried with me, and lifted me up when my face was literally in the mud.

Fenton Rhoades of alienartifacts, gave me many insightful suggestions on how to lay out the book. Gene Schwam and Joseph Trainor of Hanson and Schwam took this book under their wing and shaped it into a creative structure that was both understandable and fitting for who I am. The structure of a play, complete with acts and a programme! Gene's unwavering attention to detail led to the inclusion of the beautiful twelve paintings by Pablo Picasso that now anchor the book.

The generosity of the Pablo Picasso Estate, Artists Rights Society (ARS), and Art Resource New York, in extending the rights for the works presented is a dream come true. Playwright and screenwriter, Jeffrey Hatcher, with whose play, *A Picasso*, my love affair began, and Jack Tantleff at Paradigm, thank you so much for all the years of allowing me to produce your fabulous play.

What would a book be without a proper layout? Jonathan Miertschin has the personality of an angel and is responsible for taking the giant mess of my poetry, along with all my crazy ideas, and patiently laying it all out. In addition, he found all the other lovely images that appear in the book, helping to create the coffee table book of my dreams.

Lest we forget, how could a book exist without a cover. Thank you to Deborah Ryder of Monterey Bay Design for putting all the elements together. To the inimitable Harry Langdon, thank you for coming out of retirement to take my photo. What a team, makeup by Kelle Lynn Brown and the iconic hair stylist, Allen Edwards. Thank you for making me one of your cover girls!

To the late Patricia LaPlante-Collins, who made the ever-fateful introduction to the banker.

To my mother, who believed in me as only a mother could and to GOD, with whom everything is possible. Friends and colleagues thank you again and I'll see you all at the sequel!

Natalia Lazarus

What happens in the end?

At the end of the end...

Epilogue

You were summoned
    Into her arms
    You accepted
    And called it
    An epilogue

You said it was over
    You said you were mine
    Yet you've gone to her
    And called it
    An epilogue

continued...

A concluding part
>   Definition English Dictionary
>   So what is the concluding part
>   You said there was no turning back
>   Yet she summoned you
>   And you went right back

You obeyed
>   Like a robot in a spell
>   I demanded pray tell
>   I don't know
>   You said
>   Perhaps it's an epilogue

A speech
> Added to the end of a play
> Often giving a short statement
> About what happens to the characters
> After the play finishes
> Definition Cambridge Dictionary

What happens in the end
> At the end of the end
> The man I love
> Runs to another woman
> And calls it
> An epilogue

continued...

Going to New York
> Means a lot to her
> You said
> Didn't you see
> Not going
> Meant a lot to me

Epilogue
> A final section
> Serving as a conclusion
> To what has happened
> Definition Merriam Webster
> So what is the final section

She loved him
> Only as a free man
> Could she take him back
> He remained enchained
> She moved on
> And learned to love again

That is MY epilogue

IMAGE CREDITS

Page *viii*   Photo by François Vila

Page *xvi*   Image by alienartifacts

Page *xxvi*   Photo by James Kigin

Page *xxxiv*   Portrait photograph of Pablo Picasso, 1908, Anonymous. This work is in the public domain in the United States because it was published (or registered with the U.S. Copyright Office) before January 1, 1926. This applies to the European Union and those countries with a copyright term of 70 years after the work was made available to the public and the author never disclosed their identity.

Page *xxxviii*   Photo by Roberto Nickson from pexels.com

Page 2   Picasso, Pablo (1881 -1973) @ ARS, NY
                   Harlequin and his Companion (The Two Saltimbanques), 1901.
                   Found in the collection of the State A Pushkin Museum of Fine Arts, Moscow
                   Pushkin Museum of Fine Arts, Moscow, Russia
                   Photo Credit: HIP / Art Resource, NY
                   © 2021 Estate of Pablo Picasso / Artists Rights Society (ARS), New York

Page 4   *Exposition universelle de 1889 / État d'avancement*; Louis-Émile Durandelle (French, 1839 - 1917); Paris, France; November 23, 1888; Albumen silver print; 43.2 × 34.6 cm (17 × 13 5/8 in.); 87.XM.121.16; The J. Paul Getty Museum, Los Angeles; Rights Statement: No Copyright - United States

Page 6   Picasso, Pablo (1881 -1973) @ ARS, NY
The Dream (Le Rêve), Boisgeloup, January 24, 1932. Oil on canvas, 130 x 98 cm.
Photo Credit: Erich Lessing / Art Resource, NY
© 2021 Estate of Pablo Picasso / Artists Rights Society (ARS), New York

Page 10   *[A couple walking along the Seine River in Paris]*, [between 1940 and 1969]; Frissell, Toni, 1907-1988, photographer; digital file from b&w film negative, from Library of Congress Prints and Photographs Division Washington, D.C. 20540 USA; LCCN Permalink https://lccn.loc.gov/2013651440; No known restrictions on publication

Page 12   *Hôtel Scipion Sardini, R[ue] Scipion*; Eugène Atget (French, 1857 - 1927); Paris, France; March 1925; Albumen silver print; 17.8 × 22.2 cm (7 × 8 3/4 in.); 86.XM.23; The J. Paul Getty Museum, Los Angeles; Rights Statement: No Copyright - United States

Page 16   Picasso, Pablo (1881 -1973) @ ARS, NY
Friendship, 1907-1908.
Pushkin Museum of Fine Arts, Moscow, Russia
Photo Credit: HIP / Art Resource, NY
© 2021 Estate of Pablo Picasso / Artists Rights Society (ARS), New York

Page 18   Photo by Jean Beaufort from publicdomainpictures.net

Page 20   Photo by Stan Richards from pixabay.com

Page 24   Photo by Dean Moriarty from pixabay.com

Page 26   Photo by Melan Cholia from pixabay.com

Page 28   Photo by Hernan Pauccara from pexels.com

Page 30   ***Mer Méditerranée - Sète***, 1857; Gustave Le Gray (French, 1820–1884); Albumen silver print from two glass negatives; The Metropolitan Museum of Art, New York; Public domain

Page 32   Picasso, Pablo (1881-1973) @ ARS, NY
EL RAMO DE FLORES - 1958.
LITOGRAFIA. Author: RUIZ PICASSO, PABLO
Location: PRIVATE COLLECTION
Photo Credit: Album / Art Resource, NY
© 2021 Estate of Pablo Picasso / Artists Rights Society (ARS), New York

Page 40   Photo by Paul Henri Degrande from pixabay.com

Page 42   Picasso, Pablo (1881 -1973) @ ARS, NY
Girl before a Mirror. Boisgeloup, March 1932.
Oil on canvas, 64 x 51 ¼" (162.3 x 130.2 cm).
Gift of Mrs. Simon Guggenheim.
Digital Image @ The Museum of Modern Art/ Licensed by SCALA / Art Resource, NY
© 2021 Estate of Pablo Picasso / Artists Rights Society (ARS), New York

Page 44   Photo from photostockeditor.com

Page 46   Photo by anncapictures from pixabay.com

Page 52	Picasso, Pablo (1881 -1973) @ ARS, NY ***The Absinthe Drinker***. 1901. Oil on canvas, 73 x 54 cm. Photo Credit: Scala / Art Resource, NY © 2021 Estate of Pablo Picasso / Artists Rights Society (ARS), New York
Page 56	Photo by Daria Shevtsova from pexels.com
Page 58	Photo by cottonbro from pexels.com
Page 60	***Eternal Spring***, modeled ca. 1881, carved 1907; Auguste Rodin (French, Paris 1840–1917 Meudon); Marble; The Metropolitan Museum of Art, New York; Public domain
Page 64	Photo by James Wheeler from pexels.com
Page 72	Picasso, Pablo (1881 -1973) @ ARS, NY ***The Old Guitarist***, late 1903-early 1904. Oil on panel, 48 3/8 x 32 ½ in. (122.9 x 82.6 cm.) Helen Birch Bartlett Memorial Collection, 1926.253 Photo Credit: The Art Institute of Chicago / Art Resource, NY © 2021 Estate of Pablo Picasso / Artists Rights Society (ARS), New York
Page 74	Photo by Michael Goyberg from pexels.com
Page 76	Design for Three Chairs, Anonymous, British, early 19th century; Graphite; The Metropolitan Museum of Art, New York; Public domain
Page 80	Jewelry set, Anonymous, French, ca. 1830; Gold, amethysts; The Metropolitan Museum of Art, New York; Public domain
Page 82	Photo by Pixabay from pexels.com

Page 84   Photo by Patou Ricard from pixabay.com

Page 86   Photo by cottonbro from pexels.com

Page 88   Photo by cottonbro from pexels.com

Page 90   Picasso, Pablo (1881 -1973) @ ARS, NY
              The Weeping Woman (Femme en pleures). 1937.
              Oil on canvas, 60.8 x 50.0 cm.
              Accepted by HM Government in lieu of tax with
              additional payment (Grant-in-Aid)
              made with assistance from the National Heritage
              Memorial Fund, the Art Fund and the
              Friends of the Tate Gallery 1987.
              @ Tate, London / Art Resource, NY
              © 2021 Estate of Pablo Picasso / Artists Rights
              Society (ARS), New York

Page 92   Photo by dmorit from pixabay.com

Page 94   Picasso, Pablo (1881-1973) @ ARS, NY
              Mediterranean Landscape, 1952.
              Photo Credit: Scala / Art Resource, NY
              © 2021 Estate of Pablo Picasso / Artists Rights
              Society (ARS), New York

Page 98   Photo by Michael Shannon from unsplash.com

Page 100   Photo by Pixabay from pexels.com

Page 104   Photo by Vlada Karpovich from pexels.com

Page 108   Picasso, Pablo (1881 -1973) @ ARS, NY
              La chambre bleu (Le tub) (The Blue Room). 1901.
              Oil on canvas, 51 x 62.5 cm.
              Photo Credit: Album / Art Resource, NY
              © 2021 Estate of Pablo Picasso / Artists Rights
              Society (ARS), New York

Page 110   Photo by James Kigin

Page 112   ***Come back to me I love you so***, 1897; Florence Amiée Butler, Fort Smith, Arkansas; New York Public Library, Music Division, New York; Public domain

Page 116   ***[Fashion model underwater in dolphin tank, Marineland, Florida]***, [1939]; Frissell, Toni, 1907-1988, photographer; digital file from b&w film negative, from Library of Congress Prints and Photographs Division Washington, D.C. 20540 USA; LCCN Permalink https://www.loc.gov/resource/cph.3g06310/; No known restrictions on publication

Page 120   Basalt statue of Aphrodite, late 1st-early 2nd century A.D.; Roman; Basalt; The Metropolitan Museum of Art, New York; Public domain

Page 122   Photo by Jeremy Bishop from unsplash.com

Page 124   Photo by Maria Orlova from pexels.com

Page 126   Picasso, Pablo (1881-1973) @ ARS, NY
Moscou. 1957.
Made for the World Youth and Student Festival in Moscow, 1957.
Printed cotton. 77 x 75 cm.
Inv. 2008, 57/01. Kunstbibliothek, Staatliche Museen, Berlin, Germany
Photo Credit: bpk Bildagentur / Art Resource, NY
© 2021 Estate of Pablo Picasso / Artists Rights Society (ARS), New York

Page 128   Photo from pixabay.com

Page 130   Photo from pixabay.com

Page 130   Photo by James Kigin

Page 132   Photo by Mehdi Faez from pexels.com

Page 134   Photo by Kranich17 from pixabay.com

Page 136   Photo by MustangJoe from pixabay.com

Page 138   Photo by Hakeem James Hausley from pexels.com

Page 142   Picasso, Pablo (1881-1973) @ ARS, NY
           La toilette. 1906.
           Oil on canvas, support: 59 ½ x 39 inches (151.13 x 99.06 cm); framed:
           68 x 48 x 5 inches (172.72 x 121.92 x 12.7 cm).
           Albright Knox Art Gallery, Buffalo, New York, New York State, U.S.A.
           Photo Credit: Albright Knox Art Gallery / Art Resource, NY
           © 2021 Estate of Pablo Picasso / Artists Rights Society (ARS), New York

Page 144   Image by alienartifacts

Page 147   Affiche pour le "Champagne Jules Mumm", 1898; Réalier-Dumas, Maurice; Publisher: Imprimerie Chaix, Paris; New York Public Library, The Miriam and Ira D. Wallach Division of Art Prints and Photographs: Art & Architecture Collection, New York; Public domain

Page 148   Photo by nck_gsl from pixabay.com

Page 152   Photo by Ruth Archer from pixabay.com

www.ingramcontent.com/pod-product-compliance
Lightning Source LLC
Chambersburg PA
CBHW071812160426
43209CB00032B/1939/J